AF575373

THE BLACK AMERICAN JOURNEY

ROSA PARKS AND THE MONTGOMERY BUS BOYCOTT

"People always say that I didn't give up my seat because I was tired, but that isn't true. I was not tired physically, or no more tired than I usually was at the end of a working day. I was not old, although some people have an image of me as being old then. I was forty-two. No, the only tired I was, was tired of giving in."

— Rosa Parks (from *Rosa Parks: My Story*)

BY L.S. SUMMER

Published by The Child's World®
800-599-READ • www.childsworld.com

Content Consultant
David J. Garrow, PhD, US historian and Pulitzer Prize-winning author of *Bearing the Cross: Martin Luther King, Jr., and the Southern Christian Leadership Conference*

Photography Credits
Cover and page 4: GG Vintage Images/Newscom
Interior: US National Archives and Records Administration, 5, 25, 29 (right); AP Photo/Gene Herrick, 6, 20; Marion Post Wolcott/Library of Congress, Prints and Photographs Division, 8; Dorothea Lange/Library of Congress, Prints and Photographs Division, 9; Jack Delano/Library of Congress, Prints and Photographs Division, 11; Library of Congress, Prints and Photographs Division, 12, 28; AP Photo/Horace Cort, 13; Everett Collection/Newscom, 15, 19; AP Photo/Montgomery County Sheriff's Office, 16; AP Photo, 17, 18, 21, 22, 31; Warren K. Leffler/Library of Congress, Prints and Photographs Division, 23, 29 (left); Joe Lippincott/ZUMA Press/Newscom, 24; AP Photo/Daily Advertiser, File, 26; Bill Pugliano/ZUMA Press/Newscom, 27

ISBN Information
9781503880658 (Reinforced Library Binding)
9781503881921 (Portable Document Format)
9781503883239 (Online Multi-user eBook)
9781503884540 (Electronic Publication)

LCCN 2022949915

Printed in the United States of America

Cover and page 4 caption: Rosa Parks and Martin Luther King Jr. (in the background) worked together during the Montgomery Bus Boycott.

CONTENTS

Chapter One

A DIFFERENT TIME

The United States in the 1950s was very different than it is today. People of different skin colors were less likely to play, eat, or work together. In the South, white and Black people were separated in public places. This system was called **segregation**. It prohibited white people and Black people from such things as swimming in the same pools and drinking from the same water fountains. Public facilities had signs that read "Whites Only" and "Colored Only."

A segregated store was a common sight in the South. Jim Crow laws made discrimination legal.

Rosa Parks talks to the press before her court trial in the racial bus boycott in Montgomery, Alabama.

Some enslaved people were freed after President Abraham Lincoln signed the Emancipation Proclamation. Two presidential orders, the first in 1862 and the second in 1863, freed enslaved people in areas of the Confederacy that were still fighting against the Union during the Civil War.

Black people were freed from slavery after the US Civil War in the 1860s. However, they did not immediately gain the same rights as white people. **Racism** and **discrimination** continued to play a strong role in the treatment of Black people. When it came to housing, Black families had fewer choices. They were often forced to live in neighborhoods with less access to resources. Schools attended by Black children were poorly funded—when they were provided at all. Life was especially difficult in the South. Laws were created to keep people separated. White Americans targeted Black communities and individuals with acts of violence, including **lynching**.

Black Americans wanted to be treated with fairness and respect. Eventually groups started to talk and to meet. They organized to work for **civil rights**. Citizens—Black and white—started to demonstrate against the unfair rules.

In 1955, a 42-year-old Black seamstress named Rosa Parks took an important action that set change in motion. Her simple act—the act of saying no—became one of the major milestones on the road to equal rights in the United States.

Chapter Two

GROWING UP

Rosa Louise McCauley was born on February 4, 1913, in Tuskegee, Alabama, to James and Leona McCauley. Her mother was a well-educated schoolteacher. Her father was a carpenter who left the family when Rosa was a little girl. After James left, Leona and her two children, Rosa and Sylvester, moved back to Leona's family farm in Pine Level, Alabama, to live with Rosa's grandparents.

The only teaching job Leona could find was in another town. Leona worked and lived there during the week and went home for the weekends. When her mother was gone, Rosa spent a lot of time with her grandparents. From them, she learned the importance of education. She also developed a strong faith in God. She was taught that all people deserve fair treatment regardless of their skin color. These values remained important to Rosa throughout her life.

Students do classwork in a school for Black children in Alabama. Rosa and her brother attended segregated schools like this one.

In the South, it was common for Black children to stop going to school during harvest time so they could work in the fields.

When Rosa was a young girl, her mother taught her how to read. Rosa loved books. She also enjoyed going to school. She attended an all-Black elementary school with about 60 students. Rosa spent only five months a year in class because her elementary school was closed during harvest time. During the harvest, Black children had to help pick cotton. White children did not have to work in the fields and attended school for nine months of the year.

When Rosa was 11 years old, she went to a private school named Montgomery Industrial School. The school was founded for Black girls. The teachers at the Montgomery Industrial School taught their students the importance of dignity and self-respect. They encouraged the girls to set goals. They inspired their students to believe in themselves. Rosa loved the school and was an excellent student. She worked hard to earn money for tuition by cleaning classrooms in her spare time.

Rosa Parks wrote in her **autobiography**: "What I learned best at Miss White's school was that I was a person with dignity and self-respect, and I should not set my sights lower than anybody else just because I was black."

Some white people did not want Black children to receive an education. The Montgomery Industrial School was set on fire twice and was finally forced to close. Rosa then attended a teacher's college in Montgomery, Alabama, that operated a school for Black children. At this school, Black students could study for nine months. Before Rosa graduated, her mother and grandmother became ill. She chose to leave school after tenth grade and moved to Pine Level, Alabama, to care for them.

When Rosa was 16 years old, her grandmother died. Even though her mother's health improved, Rosa decided to stay in Pine Level. Her family needed her to manage the farm.

Soon, Rosa met a young man named Raymond Parks. Raymond shared many of Rosa's values. He did not believe in letting white people treat him unfairly. He also believed that all people should have equal rights.

Raymond and Rosa had similar experiences growing up. Raymond's father was in the building trade and left his family when Raymond was young. Education was important to Raymond. His mother taught him at home, as he could not attend the local school because he was Black. Raymond also cared for his mother when she became ill.

Raymond and Rosa fell in love. They were married in her mother's home in Pine Level on December 18, 1932. Raymond encouraged Rosa to finish high school. In 1934, she received her diploma.

Chapter Three

SEGREGATION IN THE SOUTH

The **Constitution** promises important rights to US citizens. These rights include the freedom of speech and the freedom of religion. Citizens also have the right to vote. These are called civil rights. Unfortunately, for too long, Black citizens were denied these rights.

Segregation in the South allowed a strict separation between Black and white citizens. Black children could not attend the same schools as white children. Black families could not eat in white restaurants. They could not see movies in white theaters. In Montgomery, Alabama, white people and Black people could not even play cards, checkers, or dominoes together.

Segregated bathrooms were legal in the South.

Founded in 1909, the NAACP is the nation's oldest civil rights organization.

Soon after Rosa and Raymond married, the young couple moved to Montgomery. This is where they learned about the National Association for the Advancement of Colored People (NAACP). This organization played an important role in the **civil rights movement**. The NAACP worked to help Black people gain fair treatment under the law.

In 1943, Rosa started to get involved in the civil rights movement. She joined the Montgomery chapter of the NAACP. She was elected secretary and assisted the chapter's president, E. D. Nixon. Rosa and Raymond devoted much of their time and energy to the organization. They hoped they could make a change in the South. One cause they felt strongly about was the right to vote.

Like other US citizens, all Black Americans legally held the right to vote. In order to vote, a person had to register with the government. In the South, many white people tried to keep Black citizens from registering. Sometimes they threatened Black people who tried to register. Other times, they simply turned them away. Rosa tried to register three times before she was finally successful. In 1945, Rosa was registered, yet she had to pay a **poll tax** in order to vote. After that, she voted in every election until her death.

When Rosa Parks was finally a registered voter, she had to pay a poll tax to cast her vote. In 1962, the US Congress outlawed poll taxes in federal elections.

On a segregated bus, white passengers sat in the front and Black passengers rode in the back. The law in Alabama required Black people to give up their seats to white people if the bus was full.

Black people also were treated unfairly on public buses, which had segregation rules. Black riders were often threatened or shamed when riding the buses. On Montgomery buses, Black riders had to enter through the back door. The fare box, however, was in the front. They had to use the front door to enter and pay their fare. Then they had to get off the bus, walk to the back door, and board the bus again.

The bus company employed only white drivers. Many of them were unkind or even cruel to Black passengers. Sometimes, bus drivers pulled away before Black passengers reached the back door—even after they had paid their fare.

One day in 1943, after she was turned away from registering to vote, Rosa boarded a bus at the front door and paid her fare. The bus was very crowded. Black passengers who were forced to stand blocked the rear doorway. Rosa realized there was not a good reason to get off the bus and walk to the back door. She would have to struggle to push her way through the entry. Instead, she turned down the aisle and walked directly to the back of the bus.

The bus driver ordered her to exit and enter again through the back door. Rosa patiently explained that she was already on the bus. She saw no need to get off. The driver ordered her to do as he said or get off the bus altogether. Rosa did not move.

The driver rose from his seat and walked back to where Rosa stood. He threatened her and angrily pulled on her coat sleeve. Rosa knew that he had a gun. She decided to get off the bus and wait for the next one.

Twelve years later, in 1955, segregation continued on Alabama buses. The bus drivers were required by law to enforce segregated seating. Each bus operated by Montgomery City Lines, Inc. had 36 seats. The ten seats in the front were reserved for white passengers only. Even if white people were not on the bus, Black passengers could not sit in the front seats. The ten seats in the back of the bus were reserved for Black passengers, who could sit in the middle seats only if white people were not already sitting there. Bus drivers carried weapons to make sure people did as they were told. They also had the help of police if they needed it. Not many people dared to challenge the segregation rules. If they did, they might end up in jail.

The rules that enabled segregation were called "Jim Crow laws." These laws made discrimination legal.

Rosa was arrested and fingerprinted on December 1, 1955, for violating the bus segregation law. Her friend E. D. Nixon, who was president of their local NAACP chapter, bailed Parks out of jail.

On December 1, 1955, Rosa boarded a Montgomery bus and sat down in one of the middle seats. Three other Black people sat in the same row. A white man boarded the bus after all the seats were taken. The driver told all four Black passengers in Rosa's row to stand up so that the white man could sit down. The other three seats had to remain empty. Black passengers and white passengers could not sit together in the same row.

"I had been pushed around all my life and felt at this moment that I couldn't take it anymore," Rosa Parks wrote shortly after her experience at the Montgomery city jail.

The three others got up, but Rosa stayed in her seat. She knew this was one rule that made Black people feel inferior, and she was tired of it. She was not going to get up. The bus driver told her again to give up her seat. Rosa simply said no. The driver called the police. Two police officers arrested Rosa and took her to jail. She cooperated and stayed calm throughout the humiliating process. Rosa was charged with violating the laws of segregation. She asked a police officer why they treated Black people so badly. He said he did not know. He was only following the law.

Chapter Four

THE BEGINNING OF CHANGE

The decision by Rosa Parks to stay seated showed other Black people that they could protest unfair rules. Rosa's protest caused the civil rights movement to become more active. Because of this, she is often called the "mother of the civil rights movement."

Several important things resulted from Rosa's arrest. The first was the Montgomery Bus **Boycott**. Before Rosa's trial, a group called the Women's Political Council called for action. They passed out more than 20,000 flyers asking Black residents to stay off the buses on December 5, the day of the trial, even if they had to miss a day of school or work. Word quickly spread.

Rosa Parks arrives at court during the bus boycott trial.

Before Rosa, others had been arrested for disobeying bus segregation rules. The Montgomery Bus Boycott was prompted by Rosa's arrest, however, because she was previously involved in the civil rights movement and was a well-respected citizen.

Not one Black person rode the bus in Montgomery on December 5, 1955. Some people walked or rode bikes wherever they needed to go. Others took taxis with Black drivers who charged only the price of a bus ride. Black people who owned cars shuttled others back and forth throughout the day.

At her trial on December 5, Rosa was found guilty of violating segregation laws and fined $14. This was the **verdict** E. D. Nixon and the NAACP wanted. If a US citizen is found guilty of a crime, he or she can ask a higher court to reconsider the verdict. Rosa and the NAACP then had the opportunity to take Montgomery's bus segregation law to the nation's most important court. The NAACP leaders planned to **appeal** Rosa's case before the **Supreme Court**. This was the second important result of Rosa's arrest. A year earlier, the Supreme Court had decided that it was illegal to have segregated schools. The NAACP leaders hoped the higher court would decide that bus segregation was also wrong.

Rosa Parks, E. D. Nixon, and attorney Fred Gray prepare to appeal Rosa's guilty verdict so they could argue the case before the Supreme Court.

Martin Luther King Jr. speaks at a meeting of the Montgomery Improvement Association where they decided to continue the boycott until the bus segregation rules ended.

After Rosa's trial, Montgomery's Black leaders held a meeting. They wanted to discuss if their community should continue the boycott. Every seat in the building was filled. Hundreds of people stood outside. Several people made speeches, including two local pastors named Ralph Abernathy and Martin Luther King Jr. The decision was made to continue the boycott until the bus segregation rules ended.

Black residents refused to ride Montgomery buses for 381 days—more than one year. The city's white citizens tried many things to end the boycott, including threats and acts of violence. But the **activists** did not give in. For more than a year, Black people with cars gave others rides to their destinations. Many people traveled on foot.

Brown v. Board of Education of Topeka was a landmark court case decided in 1954. Supreme Court justices ruled that segregation in schools was no longer legal.

A crowd of people packed the courthouse during the bus boycott trial. The boycott would last for more than a year.

The Montgomery police arrested many of the boycotters. Rosa was arrested a second time, this time for participating in the boycott. Rosa, King, and other leaders gave many speeches during the Montgomery Bus Boycott. They talked about the boycott and the unfairness of the South's segregation laws.

On November 13, 1956, the Supreme Court made its decision about Montgomery bus segregation. It ruled that Montgomery had to **integrate** its public bus lines. The bus company's segregation rules were now illegal. By December 21, Black passengers were free to choose where they sat on a bus. White bus drivers could no longer use the law to treat Black passengers badly. This was the third important result of Rosa's arrest. More important perhaps, everyday people realized that they had the power to change things, especially when they united as a community.

The Supreme Court decision against bus segregation could not be ignored. Unfortunately, many white people continued to believe in segregation. Some threatened those who had been involved in the bus boycott. The homes of King and Nixon were bombed. Rosa and Raymond received threatening phone calls. Rosa's mother now lived with them. Some nights, she would talk to friends on the phone all night to keep the threatening calls from coming in. The Parks family was afraid. Raymond kept a gun near him when he slept at night.

Martin Luther King Jr. is perhaps the most widely known leader of the civil rights movement. He favored nonviolent protests. In 1964, he was awarded the Nobel Peace Prize for his actions.

Ralph Abernathy (from left), Robert Graetz, and Martin Luther King Jr. were all pastors. Abernathy's and Graetz's churches were both bombed after the Supreme Court outlawed bus segregation.

Two Black men sat in the front seats of a Montgomery bus on December 21, 1956, the day the city buses were integrated.

Many Black workers lost their jobs during and after the boycott. Soon Rosa and Raymond were also out of work. They decided it was time to leave Montgomery. Rosa's brother, Sylvester, lived in Detroit, Michigan. In 1957, they moved there as well.

Rosa had become well known. She did not let moving to Detroit stop her from being active in the civil rights movement. She traveled around the country to speak about her experiences and to urge equality and justice. Meanwhile, King, Abernathy, and others had formed a new organization. They called it the Southern Christian Leadership Conference (SCLC). Its goal was to use nonviolent **civil disobedience** as a way to gain civil rights. Rosa was a supporter of the SCLC and continued to work toward making positive changes.

Chapter Five

POST-BOYCOTT ACTION

The case of Rosa Parks and the Montgomery Bus Boycott helped launch the civil rights movement. Soon, there were other boycotts. People marched in large groups throughout the South to demand better treatment. They organized freedom rides to integrate bus travel between states.

In 1963, approximately 250,000 people participated in a protest march in Washington, DC. At the time, the March on Washington was the largest demonstration in the history of the nation's capital. One main point of the event was to demonstrate that all Black Americans should be treated fairly and have equal civil rights.

Rosa Parks was very active in the civil rights movement. She attended many protests, including the March on Washington and the Poor People's Campaign in 1968 where she spoke to the crowd.

During the March on Washington, Martin Luther King Jr. gave his famous "I Have a Dream" speech at the Lincoln Memorial.

On July 2, 1964, President Lyndon Johnson signed the Civil Rights Act. It made all segregation illegal. Now the US government would stand up for the civil rights of its Black citizens. But the new law could not instantly change people's beliefs or behavior. Black Americans still faced discrimination. Rosa Parks knew there was much more to be done.

In 1965, Rosa became an assistant to a Black congressman, Representative John Conyers of Michigan. Rosa respected his views and ideas. She worked for Conyers until she retired in 1988.

The 1970s brought difficult times for Rosa. Raymond died in 1977. Her brother, Sylvester, died three months later. Rosa's mother moved to a nursing home because her health continued to fail. Rosa visited her mother three times each day. In 1978, Rosa moved her mother back home to care for her. Her mother died the following year.

After John Conyers was elected to Congress in 1964, he hired Rosa Parks as a member of his staff at his office in Detroit.

President Bill Clinton awards Rosa Parks the Presidential Medal of Freedom in 1996. It is the highest award a civilian can receive from the government.

In 1987, Rosa and her close friend Elaine Steele founded the Rosa and Raymond Parks Institute for Self-Development. The organization offers education and community programs to young people between the ages of 11 and 18. Youth education was always very important to Rosa. The organization also awards scholarships to Black students.

One program at the institute is called Pathways to Freedom. Children in the program have the chance to travel across the United States tracing the path of the **Underground Railroad**. They also visit the scenes of important events in the civil rights movement.

Rosa received many awards and honors for her work in civil rights. Some of these include the Eleanor Roosevelt Women of Courage Award (1984), the Presidential Medal of Freedom (1996), and the International Freedom Conductor Award (1998).

There have been other tributes to Rosa's courage as well. The city of Montgomery, Alabama, has named a street after her. Hundreds of other roads, schools, and parks around the country bear her name. The Rosa Parks Library and Museum was founded at Troy University in Montgomery. It helps people understand the events that led to the famous bus boycott.

Rosa Parks died on October 25, 2005, at the age of 92. In 2013, a bronze statue of Rosa Parks was installed in the US Capitol Building. President Barack Obama, the first Black American president, spoke at the dedication ceremony. He talked about Rosa's courage and how her actions helped spark a movement that changed the country. "Rosa Parks tells us there's always something we can do," Obama said. "She tells us that we all have responsibilities, to ourselves and to one another. She reminds us that this is how change happens."

Rosa sat in the front of a Montgomery bus on December 21, 1956, after the Supreme Court ordered the bus system to be integrated.

"I would like to be known as a person who is concerned about freedom and equality," Parks wrote, "and justice and prosperity for all people."

Throughout her life, Rosa Parks worked for equality and justice. She seemed to touch everyone she met, from children to senior citizens. Rosa believed that intelligence and self-respect are powerful weapons against **prejudice**. She is proof that the act of one person can change the world. Today, her life continues to inspire many people to demand equality.

Rosa Parks was the first woman and first nongovernment official to lie in honor in the Rotunda of the US Capitol in Washington, DC.

THINK ABOUT IT

Why is the Montgomery Bus Boycott an important part of US history?
In your opinion, why should we still talk about it today?

Rosa Parks and Martin Luther King Jr. believed that nonviolent civil disobedience was the best way to fight against discrimination.
Do you agree or disagree? What are some strengths and weaknesses of peaceful protesting?

TIME LINE

1910

1913
Rosa McCauley is born in Tuskegee, Alabama, on February 4.

1918
Rosa starts school in Pine Level, Alabama.

1920–1930

1924
Rosa attends school in Montgomery, Alabama.

1929
Rosa leaves school to care for her grandmother.

1932
Rosa marries Raymond Parks.

1934
Rosa receives her high school diploma.

1940–1950

1943
Rosa joins the NAACP and is elected secretary of the Montgomery chapter.

1955
Rosa is arrested on December 1 for violating the bus segregation law. On December 5, Black residents of Montgomery begin boycotting the bus system.

1956
On January 30, Martin Luther King Jr.'s home is bombed. E. D. Dixon's home is bombed the day after. On February 21, Rosa is arrested a second time for participation in the Montgomery Bus Boycott. On November 13, the Supreme Court declares the laws requiring segregated buses to be illegal.

1957
Rosa and her family move to Detroit, Michigan.

Rosa Parks and Martin Luther King Jr. are just two of many civil rights leaders who dedicated their lives to fighting for equality.
Can you name another leader in the civil rights movement? What is he or she most known for?

What are some modern-day protests or demonstrations? What form did they take?
In other words, were they marches, boycotts, or some other type of protest? Were those protests effective? Do they have anything in common with the Montgomery Bus Boycott?

1960

1963
Rosa participates in the March on Washington for Jobs and Freedom.

1964
President Lyndon Johnson signs the Civil Rights Act on July 2.

1965
Rosa joins the staff of Representative John Conyers.

1970-1980

1977
Rosa's brother and husband, Raymond, both die of cancer.

1979
Rosa's mother dies.

1987
Rosa founds the Rosa and Raymond Parks Institute for Self-Development.

1988
Rosa retires from John Conyers's staff.

1990-2010

1992
Rosa Parks: My Story is published.

1996
President Bill Clinton presents Rosa with the Presidential Medal of Freedom.

2000
The Rosa L. Parks Library and Museum opens at Troy University in Montgomery, Alabama.

2005
Rosa dies on October 25 at the age of 92.

2013
A statue of Rosa Parks is unveiled in the US Capitol. The statue depicts Rosa sitting down, wearing the clothes she wore when she was arrested. It is the first full-length statue of a Black American in the Capitol.

GLOSSARY

activists (AK-tih-vists)
An activist is someone who takes direct action for a particular cause. Rosa and Raymond Parks were inspired to become activists to fight for equality.

appeal (uh-PEEL)
Attempting to change a court's decision by asking a higher court to consider the case is called an appeal. Rosa Parks challenged her court verdict with an appeal.

autobiography (aw-toh-bye-OG-ruh-fee)
An autobiography is when an author writes a book about his or her own life.

boycott (BOY-kot)
Not using a certain product or service as a form of protest is called a boycott. The Montgomery Bus Boycott protested segregation on Montgomery buses.

civil disobedience (SIV-ul diss-uh-BEE-dee-uhns)
Civil disobedience is disobeying government laws in order to protest them. The Southern Christian Leadership Conference (SCLC) used civil disobedience to protest racism and discrimination.

civil rights (SIV-il RYTS)
Civil rights are personal freedoms that belong to all citizens. Black Americans protested to fight for civil rights and equality.

civil rights movement (SIV-il RITES MOOV-muhnt)
The struggle for equal rights for Black people in the United States during the 1950s and 1960s is often called the civil rights movement. Martin Luther King Jr. was a leader of the civil rights movement.

Constitution (kon-stuh-TOO-shun)
The Constitution is the written document containing the principles by which the United States is governed. The Supreme Court rules on cases based on the US Constitution.

discrimination (diss-krim-ih-NAY-shun)
Discrimination is unfair treatment of people based on differences of race, gender, religion, or culture.

integrate (IN-tuh-grayt)
To combine different things together into one group is to integrate them. A goal of the Montgomery Bus Boycott was to end unfair treatment of Black passengers on Montgomery buses.

lynching (LINCH-ing)
Lynching is putting a person to death by hanging without legal cause. In the South, the lynching of Black citizens was a crime that often went unpunished.

poll tax (POHL TAKS)
A poll tax is a fixed amount of money that potential voters are required to pay before voting. Rosa Parks had to pay a poll tax in order to vote.

prejudice (PREJ-uh-diss)
A negative feeling or opinion about someone without just cause is prejudice.

racism (RAY-sih-zum)
Racism is the belief that one race is superior to another. Rosa Parks and other Black people experienced racism from white people.

segregation (seg-ruh-GAY-shun)
The act of keeping race, class, or ethnic groups apart is called segregation. Before the Supreme Court ruling against it, segregation was legal on Montgomery buses.

Supreme Court (suh-PREEM KORT)
The Supreme Court is the most powerful court in the United States. A Supreme Court decision ended school segregation.

Underground Railroad (UN-dur-ground RAYL-rohd)
The Underground Railroad was a network of people who helped enslaved people escape before the US Civil War. Through the Rosa and Raymond Parks Institute for Self-Development, children can follow one such path on the Underground Railroad.

verdict (VUR-dikt)
A verdict is a decision by a jury stating if a person is guilty or not guilty of a crime. At Rosa Parks's first trial on December 5, 1955, she received a guilty verdict.

FURTHER INFORMATION

BOOKS

Cooper, Brittney, and Cathy Ann Johnson (illustrator). *Stand Up! 10 Mighty Women Who Made a Change*. New York, NY: Orchard Books, 2022.

Fitzpatrick, Insha, and Abelle Hayford (illustrator). *Who Sparked the Montgomery Bus Boycott?* New York, NY: Penguin Workshop, 2021.

Leslie, Tonya, and Charnelle Pinkney Barlow (illustrator). *So Other People Would Be Free: The Real Story of Rosa Parks for Kids*. Emeryville, CA: Rockridge Press, 2019.

Miller, Rann. *Resistance Stories from Black History for Kids: Inspiring People and Events That Every Kid Should Know*. Berkeley, CA: Ulysses Press, 2023.

Santella, Andrew. *The NAACP*. Mankato, MN: The Child's World, 2022.

Venable, Rose. *The Civil Rights Movement*. Mankato, MN: The Child's World, 2021.

WEBSITES

Visit our website for links about Rosa Parks and the Montgomery Bus Boycott:

childsworld.com/links

Note to Parents, Caregivers, Teachers, and Librarians: We routinely verify our Web links to make sure they are safe, active sites—so encourage your readers to check them out!

INDEX